Old Seahouses

Katrina Porteous

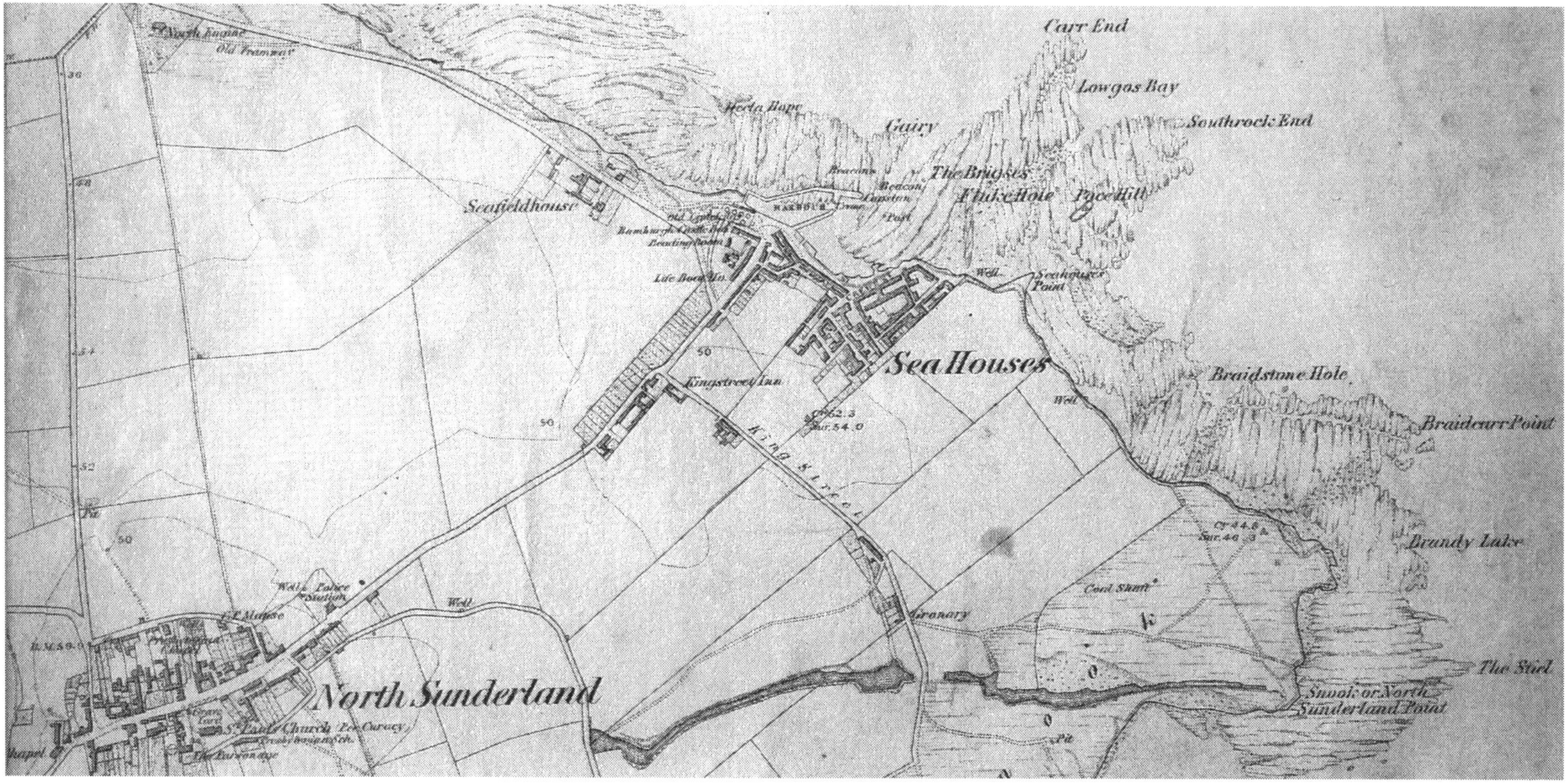

This extract from the first edition six-inch scale Ordnance Survey map *c.*1866 shows North Sunderland and Seahouses as two separate settlements. The 1780s harbour was approached through a narrow rock gully, marked by beacons on either side. A wider entrance was later blasted through the rock when the new harbour was built in the 1880s. Besides fishing, the main employment of the settlement was farming, quarrying and lime-burning, coastal trading and grain shipping. The map shows limestone quarries stretching inland from the Snook on either side of King Street, coal shafts on the links, and a granary just north of the quarries.

Text © Katrina Porteous, 2014.
First published in the United Kingdom, 2014,
by Stenlake Publishing Ltd.
01290 551122
www.stenlake.co.uk

Printed by
P2D Books, 1 Newlands Rd, Westoning, Bedford MK45 5LD

ISBN 9781840336825

The publishers regret that they cannot supply copies of any pictures featured in this book.

Acknowledgements

I would like to thank Alan Glen of the Olde Ship Hotel, Seahouses, for suggesting this book and providing most of the pictures, and Geoffrey Stewart, Seahouses historian, for generously supplying much of the information. Thanks also to Catherine Petty for additional pictures, to the late Andrew Rutter for information, and to Harry Beamish, John and Kathleen Dixon, George Dawson and David Donaldson for further information and corrections. Any remaining mistakes are, of course, my own.

Further Reading

A Seahouses Saga; Andrew Craig Rutter (Stockport 1998)
Clarty Boots and Inky Fingers; ed. Katrina Porteous (Old Parish of Bamburgh Archive Group 2007).
St. Paul's Church North Sunderland; David W. Donaldson (2007)
Walks around the Old Grain Ports of Northumberland; ed. Tony Barrow (Northumberland Co. Library 1995)
The Bonny Fisher Lad; ed. Katrina Porteous (The People's History 2003)
Ports and Harbours of Northumberland; Stafford Linsley (Tempus 2005)

Seahouses Harbour packed with Scottish herring keelboats, or 'Fifies', *c.*1900.

Introduction

The title 'Old Seahouses' comprises two distinct settlements, North Sunderland and Seahouses. The older settlement was Sutherlannland, meaning the southern lands of the Bamburgh estate, which was part of the royal estates until the reign of Elizabeth I. The prefix 'North' was added to avoid confusion with the much larger Sunderland on the Wear. Before the late 18th century, fishermen tended to live a little way inland, and the fishermen of North Sunderland and Shoreston fished from the sandy Monks' House haven rather than from rocky Seahouses. With the introduction from Scotland of more industrialised methods of herring fishing, however, many coastal villages developed 'sea houses'; and at 'North Sunderland Sea Houses' the population increased so rapidly that the name stuck.

People have lived in the Seahouses area for thousands of years: Bronze Age burials and pottery were discovered near the Manor House, North Sunderland, in 1862, and on the present Seafield caravan site when the reservoir was built in 1905. From the 18th century the village developed under the eye of its major landowners, the Lord Crewe Estates. Lord Crewe, Bishop of Durham, acquired the former royal estates of Bamburgh from the Forster family in the late 17th century, and when he died without an heir in 1720, a charitable trust was formed, and the profits used for philanthropic purposes. The main industries which shaped Seahouses in the 18th and early 19th centuries were quarrying, lime-burning and grain export. The first harbour was built to serve the limekilns, which were supplied from quarries on Snook Point, and by coal pits from north and south of the village. By the 1830s, however, the summer herring industry had begun to dominate the harbour, and the activities of the Ewing family who organised that industry influenced the village for much of the next century.

The picture on the page opposite, c.1900, shows the impact of the herring industry at its height. The harbour is packed with Scottish herring keelboats, or 'Fifies'. Herring is a migratory fish, and shoals travel down the North Sea coast from Shetland in January to East Anglia in autumn, reaching their spawning grounds between late May and September. In the hey-day of herring fishing, large fleets of drifters followed the shoals, fishing overnight when the herring rose to feed, hunting them by the 'fire' of their phosphorescence in the water, then landing their catch as quickly as possible the next morning at the nearest port. By the mid 19th century, Seahouses had become a major herring port, and was known as the 'Yarmouth of the North'. During those summer months, the village teemed with life. As late as September 20th 1901, the *Berwick Advertiser* reported: 'Over 100 boats arrived on Thursday ... During the afternoon several Scotch boats arrived very heavily fished, 50-120 crans.' A cran weighed about 28 stone and averaged around 1,200 fish. 19,263 crans of fresh herring and 2,687 tons of cured herring were exported from Seahouses in 1903.

This book concentrates on the half century from that time to 1950, a period of rapid change. After the First World War, which saw the end of the 'sailing days', both Seahouses and Scottish boats continued to land herring for processing in the village. In contrast, North Sunderland retained a distinctly agricultural character. Today the name 'Seahouses' generally refers to both settlements. Since the Second World War, both herring fishing and white fishing have ended here, and although some fishing for crabs and lobsters continues, the economic basis of Seahouses has shifted dramatically to the holiday and tourist trade. The character of the settlement has changed greatly, from two tightly-knit communities where everyone knew one another, and shared a common purpose, to one more loosely-connected village, with a fluctuating population of around 1,800, a figure which is greatly augmented by summer holidaymakers. Visitors are attracted by the beaches and the wildlife sanctuary of the Farne Islands, but also by the 'feel' of a traditional fishing village, which the older parts of Seahouses retain, and which this book explores.

Left: A red-sailed herring keelboat leaves harbour with additional power from oars, *c*.1905. A steam tug was sometimes used to help sailing keelboats get underway. The hexagonal lighthouse and flag signal on the north pier can be seen between the two 'leading marks' which, when lined up, showed the way into the harbour.

Packing herring *c*.1903. This picture shows barrels stacked on 'Lifeboat Hill' to the north of the harbour, where the lifeboat house now stands, and in what is now a car park above it. Herring yard owner, Peter Boston, stands far right. As soon as the keelboats arrived in harbour, merchants bid for the herring. They then carted them off to one of about a dozen processing yards in the village, where they were sorted and gutted by local women, together with 'Gallics', women who travelled from Scotland following the herring shoals. Herring is an oily fish, quick to spoil, and before refrigeration there were several ways of processing them, using salt or smoke. 'Cured' herring for export were salted and carefully packed, inspected and stamped with the Crown Brand by the yard's overseer, or 'cooper'. Each barrel held about 1,000 herring and the record for a team from Seahouses was 24 barrels in one day. Here, barrels wait for ships to export them to ports such as Danzig and Stettin on the Baltic. On September 13th 1901 the *Berwick Advertiser* reported that 'the steamer *Clara* sailed for the continent on Wednesday with nearly 2,000 barrels of cured herring, the first shipment of the season.'

Seahouses Harbour was built in several stages. A narrow gully in the rocks formed a natural haven, and the first harbour was a quay with a wooden jetty serving the granaries. This is depicted in a painting on display in Bamburgh Castle. In the 1780s the Lord Crewe Trustees paid Robert Cramond of Dunbar to build a stone harbour. Much of that now forms the inner harbour, seen here c.1908. Partly obscured by two herring keelboats in the harbour, a barge and pontoon can be seen (centre) with what is probably a drilling rig for harbour repairs. Three smaller Northumbrian 'cobles' lie further inside the harbour. Although keelboats were favoured for herring fishing, cobles were used throughout the rest of the year for line fishing for white fish such as cod and haddock, netting for salmon, and for potting for crabs and lobsters. They also carried visitors to the Farne Islands. This picture shows the funnel of a steam tug (left), used to tow a stone lighter and sailing keelboats out to sea, and the harbour office (right), with the weigh-bridge in front of it. The cobbled surface of the road is clearly visible. The outer harbour, also visible, was added in 1886-9 to accommodate the growing number of keelboats during the herring season. Five times larger than its predecessor, it included the north pier with its lighthouse, and an eastern breakwater, and cost £31,000.

A view of the harbour from the south, c.1935, showing the old stonework of the inner pier. The north end of the fish quay in the foreground, where merchants bid for fish daily at the auction, or 'bell', contains some of the earliest stonework of the harbour. The coble on the beach, though motorised, represents an ancient tradition. Having no proper keel, a coble did not require a harbour, and most Northumbrian harbours were built to serve industries other than fishing. Before the quay was built in the 1780s, the beach stretched to the doors of the 18th century cottages (centre). The three-storey houses (left) were originally early 19th century granaries belonging to the Lord Crewe Estates and leased to John Railston, a wealthy Seahouses grain merchant. Railston's trade benefited from the collapse of Alnmouth as a commercial port in 1806, and from the protection of the Corn Laws (1815-46), which placed a duty on imported corn. In 1846-47 31 vessels carried more than 1,000 tons of grain from Seahouses. The repeal of the Corn Laws, which only came into full effect in 1849, combined with the coming of the railways, ended the grain export boom at Seahouses.

Cramond's 1780s harbour became the inner harbour 100 years later. Its outer pier, the shape of which is still visible here as the middle pier within the 1880s harbour, was built to withstand the full force of the sea. Its stone face sloped to resist breakers. Loading facilities were from the end of the short inner pier, or opposite the kilns. The 'battlement', or high wall on Cramond's outer pier, was removed in 1903. This photograph, taken shortly afterwards, shows the harbour houses in the background and, behind them, a row of old farm cottages known as 'Hound's Ditch'. The 1866 Ordnance Survey map shows Cramond's outer pier culminating in a clublike end, accommodating a capstan which was used to manoeuvre sailing vessels in and out of harbour. A 'low light' (lantern) was lit at the end of the pier, with the 'high light' at the gable end at the top of the Mally Stairs, which led down from Chapel Row to the harbour. The two brought into line were the marks for entering the harbour. Fishermen later navigated using the gable of the Methodist chapel (background, left). The mouth of Cramond's harbour was narrower than the present inner harbour, and during heavy seas it could be shut with booms which were dropped down a slot in each pier end and lifted out using a small crane.

Looking west from the harbour towards the Bamburgh Castle Inn, c.1898. In the foreground, cobles lie at moorings; to the left stand fishermen's cottages, a hut belonging to the fish buyer John Ross, and the harbour master's office and weigh-bridge. Above them, on the hill, a horse and trap unloads outside the Ship Inn, with Willy Graham's grocery store behind it. The building to its left is a separate property, and to the left of that are two shops, which had recently burned down. The building which is now the Bamburgh Castle Hotel was originally partly a granary. It belonged to the Lord Crewe Estate, which also owned the harbour and much of the land in the village. At the time of this picture, the Bamburgh Castle Inn occupied only the farthest right part of the building, whilst the rest housed an infants' school, surgery and dispensary, a shop, and a mission for shipwrecked sailors, all provided by the Lord Crewe's philanthropic trust. There was also a reading room on the first floor, intended to keep fishermen out of the ale-houses. The Lord Crewe Estate is still a major landowner at Seahouses.

This picture, taken about 30 years later, shows alterations to the Bamburgh Castle Inn, now an hotel. The road that runs in front of it continues to the old farm cottages (centre). The building to the left of the cottages has been extended, and houses Charlie 'Buttony' Dawson and his daughter Madge's General Dealers' shop. According to fisherman Andrew Rutter, the shop sold 'everything: groceries, bullets (sweets), Woodbines, cutch, tows (ropes), lines and gear for the Scottish boats'. 'Cutch' was a brown vegetable substance, catechu, imported from Indonesia and used to 'bark', or size and preserve, fishing gear: hence the red-brown sails of the keelboats. It was chopped up in the shop using a guillotine. Madge's shop occupied the front room of the house; meat-hooks hung between it and the room behind it.

The original 'North Sunderland Sea Houses', c.1900. Those on the right, built to house lime-workers, date from the mid 18th century. The wooden porches shelter steps leading to the upper storey. Before the quay was built in the 1780s, these cottages opened onto the shore and the ground floor, used mainly for storage, was liable to flood. When Walter White, writing in 1858, described Seahouses as: 'A small, common-looking town, squalid in places, with shops that are also living rooms and bedrooms, and a general appearance of not caring very much for the fitness of things,' he was describing such houses. Behind them (right) is the row of former farm cottages. The old Methodist chapel (background, centre) stands near the top of the Mally Stairs, between the two and three-storey cottages. These were called after Mary 'Mally' Carr, an old unmarried woman who, in the mid 19th century, kept a grocery shop in the tall house at their foot. In this picture the house has a paraffin stall outside. The group (centre, *left to right*) includes Harry, Nellie and Thomasina Allen and Meggie Hanson. The three-storey houses (left) had been John Railston's granaries. Grain was loaded from the top, on what is now Chapel Row. The eye of a grain-drying kiln can still be seen farther up the hill (out of shot). The granaries fell into disuse in the mid 19th century, and were converted into houses for fishermen. They are now mostly holiday homes.

Mary Ann and Willie Greshon, baiting a long line, c.1920. The fishermen's year was divided between the summer herring season and, from October to March, fishing with long lines for white fish such as cod, haddock and ling. Fishermen used cobles for long lining, and each man carried about a mile of line, from which were suspended c.1,400 'hyeuks' (hooks) baited with mussels and limpets. The job of collecting bait and baiting the lines fell to the women, who were an indispensible and largely unpaid part of the family fishing economy. The task required great expertise: the line was coiled in a wicker 'swull', and the 'sneeyds' from which the hyeuks were suspended arranged in rows on straw to prevent them tangling. Lines were usually baited indoors in winter, at the kitchen table. The arduous nature of the work was difficult for women not brought up to it, and was a major reason for a fisherman to marry within his own community. Another of the women's tasks was the knitting of fisher 'ganseys' or jerseys, like the one Willie is wearing in this picture. There were no patterns, and each woman's handiwork was so distinctive that a drowned fisherman could be identified by his gansey.

The beach south of the harbour, looking towards Braeside (now Crewe Street), c.1929. Fish are ferried by skiff from coble *Morning Star* BK 255, then transferred to carts to be carried to the fish merchant. Behind the cart is a channel mark known as the 'Gairy Pole', and in the background (right) two yawls lie beneath what was originally the 'Coble Gut': a gap in the bank where boats were drawn up. This was filled in, and the Ewings' two herring yards built on top of it, in the mid 19th century. A wall marks the old opening. Alexander Ewing, a stern Presbyterian, moved to the village from Horncliffe in 1828 as head of a curing firm from Eyemouth. He quickly set up his own business, and he and his brother Andrew built much of the property between Crewe Street and South Street, including Alexander's family home, Horncliffe House, on Union Street. At the far left of the picture is a yard which belonged in the 1920s to the Archbold family, originally from Craster. They too moved to Seahouses to invest in the expanding herring industry. At the centre is Smith's herring yard. Centre right is the row of Coastguard cottages with their clear view north. H.M. Coastguard was founded in 1822 from the amalgamation of three services, initially to prevent smuggling. It soon became important in a lifesaving capacity. A Coastguard was stationed in Seahouses from at least 1841, and from 1851 three and sometimes four Coastguards are listed in the census. In 1901 there was still no telephone in the village, and flags were used to signal to vessels at sea. The cottage with a flagpole at the eastern end of the row was the Coastguard watch-house, with the Coastguard boathouse behind it. The house on the western end of this row included, in the 19th century, the first bank in Seahouses.

Looking north from the harbour, c.1905. In the background (left) is Seafield Farm, now a caravan site and apartment complex. The tall chimney belonged to a steam threshing engine. In 1844 Seafield was the site of a scandal, when young Rachel Skelly, heiress to the lime business, wed James Belaney, supposedly a doctor, from Ayton. Belaney had ambitious plans to rejuvenate his wife's family business. When first her widowed mother, then Rachel herself, died shortly afterwards in London, suspicions were aroused. Belaney was charged with poisoning his wife, but acquitted on lack of evidence. He returned to Seahouses in September 1844, provoking a riot in which his effigy was set on fire and Seafield House looted and burned down. To the right of the farm is the harbour master's house (since demolished) and, behind that, the water tower with its pump-house. On the shore below Seafield a spring-fed stone cistern marks the source of the first reliable water supply in the village. The pump-house eventually became a private electricity generating station, which operated until 1928, when mains electricity came to Seahouses. In the early 19th century the road north had also been the route of a horse-drawn tramway, bringing coal for the limekilns from the North Engine pit. To the left, above the herring barrels, stand 'the bothies', built for the Lord Crewe Estate's harbour extension in the 1880s. The shed in the foreground belonged to fish buyer George Edington. Next to it, near the site of the present lifeboat house, stand a number of cobles. From 1947 until the early 1990s, R. Dawson and Sons' boat-building yard occupied this site, producing many traditional wooden boats of this kind.

The harbour from the north, c.1930, showing the outline of the 1880s pier and breakwater, with the lighthouse (left). The squat building in the foreground housed public 'netties' (privvies), which emptied straight over the harbour wall into the sea. The north end of the limekilns, open in this picture behind the cobles, was later closed off and the Trinity House store built next to it in the 1950s. Around 1930 the breakwater, known locally as 'the Gantry', was breached by the sea, as can be seen here. To its right, out among the rocks on Pace Hill, stands a small sandstone building, the 'Poother Hoose' (Powder House) or magazine, which was used to store the explosives needed to cut through the rocks during the building of the breakwater. It is now a listed building. Outside the harbour (left) is a steam drifter, a type of fishing boat which signalled the end of herring fishing for many Northumbrian villages. Steam drifters, introduced c.1880, proliferated in the East Coast fleet before the First World War. Motor boats were also introduced in the early 1900s. Steam drifters were too big for smaller, tidal harbours, and required too much investment for Seahouses fishermen; so most local families sold or abandoned their sailing keelboats, converted their cobles to motor, and after the First World War acquired small double-ended motor boats called 'mules' or 'yawls', which they used both for herring fishing and for small-scale seine-netting.

Another view of the harbour from about the same time. The 1880s pier and lighthouse (left), breached breakwater (centre, showing the posts with which it was reinforced when first built), and Powder House (right) are clearly visible. This is a typical summer scene, with fleets of 'creeves' (crab and lobster pots) on the piers, and a number of Scottish herring Fifies which have been converted from sail to motor. Seahouses had very few motorised Fifies, and none at all by this time. Charles Dawson's *Speedwell* BK 174 was the last. Here, the Trinity House boat *Grace Darling* (left), and motor cobles and salmon boats are moored in the inner harbour. The double-ended 'mule' with a wheelhouse (centre right) is Ned and George Dawson's *Blossom* BK40, and is typical of the boats used by Seahouses fishermen between the wars.

Cobles and mules in the harbour in the 1930s. The mules include Jim Robson's *Respect* BK162, Charlie Dawson's *Providence* BK142 (with wheelhouses, centre back), Ned Dawson's *Blossom* BK40 and Bill 'Cloggy' Robson's *Favourite* (middle, *left to right*). The picture shows a thriving fishing harbour, but the brooding bulk of the limekilns (right), used here as fishermen's stores, reminds us that industries come and go. The Lord Crewe Trustees first allowed John Pringle and James Blackett to build kilns here in 1768. Others were built along the shore to the north. In the early 19th century the harbour kilns, operated by Robson and Skelly, expanded to four pots, which were fired to temperatures over 1,000 degrees centigrade. The quicklime fell to the base of the kiln and was raked out, cooled, then loaded onto sailing ships or 'sloops'. A wooden shelter projected from the kilns, shielding the volatile lime, which could catch fire if it got wet. Lime was exported to Scotland as an agricultural fertiliser, and shipments from Seahouses peaked in 1848. But the coming of the railway, together with difficulty with coal supplies, meant that, for Seahouses, the boom was short-lived. In 1858 orders were issued to close down the industry, and the kilns were last fired that year. At the time of this picture there were steps just south of the limekilns, and the top of the kilns, which belonged to the Coastguard, was used as a flag and semaphore signal station, communicating daily with Longstone. It is now a pub garden.

In the early 1930s, as seen on p.15, the outer breakwater was breached by the sea. The Lord Crewe Trustees were unable to meet the expense of its repair, so the Ministry of Agriculture and Fisheries took over the harbour and appointed Commissioners to act on its behalf. The Commissioners include members of Northumberland County Council, three representatives elected by the local fishermen and one by the Crewe Trustees. The pictures show the damage to the breakwater, the railway which was constructed to move materials for its repair, and the steam crane lowering concrete blocks into position. These interlocking blocks, which were made on North Sunderland Point, were used to straighten and lengthen the breakwater, in order to lessen the 'run' of heavy seas coming into the harbour. The repairs, undertaken by Clerk of Works Basil Palmer and a firm called Holloway who also built the new bridge at Berwick, took place between 1932 and '34, and cost approximately £22,000. Since then, many further costly repairs to the harbour and breakwater have been necessary, including, in 2003, £600,000 worth of emergency repairs to the middle and inner piers and, in 2008, repairs to the outer pier and further major work on the breakwater, which is now encased in concrete.

Methodism was very important to the development of Seahouses. Evangelists William Dunn and Andrew Taylor first brought it to the village when they visited on holiday in 1867, and the faith still remains central to many fishermen, exposed as they often are to danger at sea. This picture from September 1950 shows Seahouses fishermen during a visit from former minister, Prof. Norman Snaith (centre right). *Back row, left to right*: Charlie 'Tinyen' Dawson, George Dawson Sr, Jimmy Walker, George Robson, Rev. J.V. Staton, unknown, Johnnie Archbold, Prof. N. Snaith, George 'Dode' Nelson, Tom Baxter Douglas, George Nelson, Charlie Dawson. *Front row, left to right*: Tom Dawson, Herbert Gallagher, Mick Robson, Bobby Douglas, Bobby Greshon, George Dawson Jr, Bill 'Cloggy' Robson.

Three Seahouses fishermen, Jimmy Galoney (left), Jack 'Dobbin' Robson and Robert Bertram (obscured), mend their 'creeves' (crab pots) on the pier c.1938. Between them, at moorings, lie two vessels; *Mary*, an old lifeboat from Seaham, converted to a pleasure boat by Tom Swallow, and Charlie Dawson's mule, *Providence* BK142. Over the centuries, fishermen have always needed to adapt, and in Seahouses since the Second World War this has increasingly meant balancing the demands of the leisure industry with fishing. Throughout the long history of herring fishing until its demise in the 1970s, Seahouses fishermen also continued to catch white fish, using long lines until the war, then seine nets, and from the late 1960s, otter-trawl nets. For a few years, about ten small trawlers fished out of Seahouses; but over-fishing by larger boats from major ports, combined with EU regulations, led to the end of this type of fishing. Now there is only one Seahouses boat over 10 metres, which fishes mainly out of Scottish ports. A dozen or so small boats still fish from Seahouses, catching mainly crabs and lobsters, and some also take out angling parties or divers. The majority of boats in the harbour today are not fishing boats but vessels specially designed to take trips to the Farne Islands.

The Express, Seahouses. 5405

Seahouses Station stood on the site of the present car park and Tourist Information Centre. The North Eastern Railway Co. refused to provide a branch line to travel the four miles from Seahouses to Chathill on the main East Coast railway; so a group of local merchants and fishermen formed their own company. In August 1898 they opened a private line. The main purpose was to transport fish to market, but the line opened to passengers soon afterwards. It reflected the prosperity which herring had brought to Seahouses, and contributed significantly to the development of the tourist trade. The line was operated by a single saddle tank engine named *Bamburgh*, with five carriages. The Light Railways Act imposed a speed restriction of 16 mph, so the caption, 'the Express', is a joke. The crane in the background, used for loading, previously stood on Seahouses Pier. In August 1924 three wagons broke loose and careered through the corrugated iron engine shed, to the old herring yards across the road. Fortunately, no one was hurt. In 1934 a small diesel electric locomotive was added, named the *Lady Armstrong*. Both locomotives survived the Second World War, but the line was rarely profitable and closed in 1951. It is still remembered fondly by older locals, who refer to it as 'the Tanky'.

Returning the lifeboat to the lifeboat house beside the present Neptune restaurant, c.1920. The lifeboat was largely hauled by manpower, though horses from Seafield Farm were used on the hill and when it was needed farther afield. The sound of 'maroons' (rockets) summoned everyone in the village and, with many able-bodied men at sea, women were often called to help launch it. The boat in this picture is the *Forster Fawsett* (1906-25), which was launched 56 times and saved 123 lives. Uniformed sea cadets help tow it, suggesting that this was perhaps a show event. Behind the boat lies a derelict herring yard (left) and the back of the Bamburgh Castle Hotel (right), all Lord Crewe Estate property. Among the outbuildings in the hotel courtyard was a fire-pump house on the south side. This picture dates from before the War Memorial (overleaf). In the early 19th century, Robson and Skelly's rope-drawn railway from their Snook Point quarry would have run across the centre of this picture to the top of the limekilns. Between the wars, the herring yard (now MacKay's Farne Gift Shop) became Davey Allen's sweet shop and barber's and, upstairs, C.W. Park's Farne Island booking office. Later it became MacKay's fishmonger's. To its left, out of shot, stood the Castle Garage, from which Tom Bolton ran one of the first bus services in the area. For 30 years, from the early 1970s, the Viking Ballroom and arcades complex occupied the site where apartments now stand.

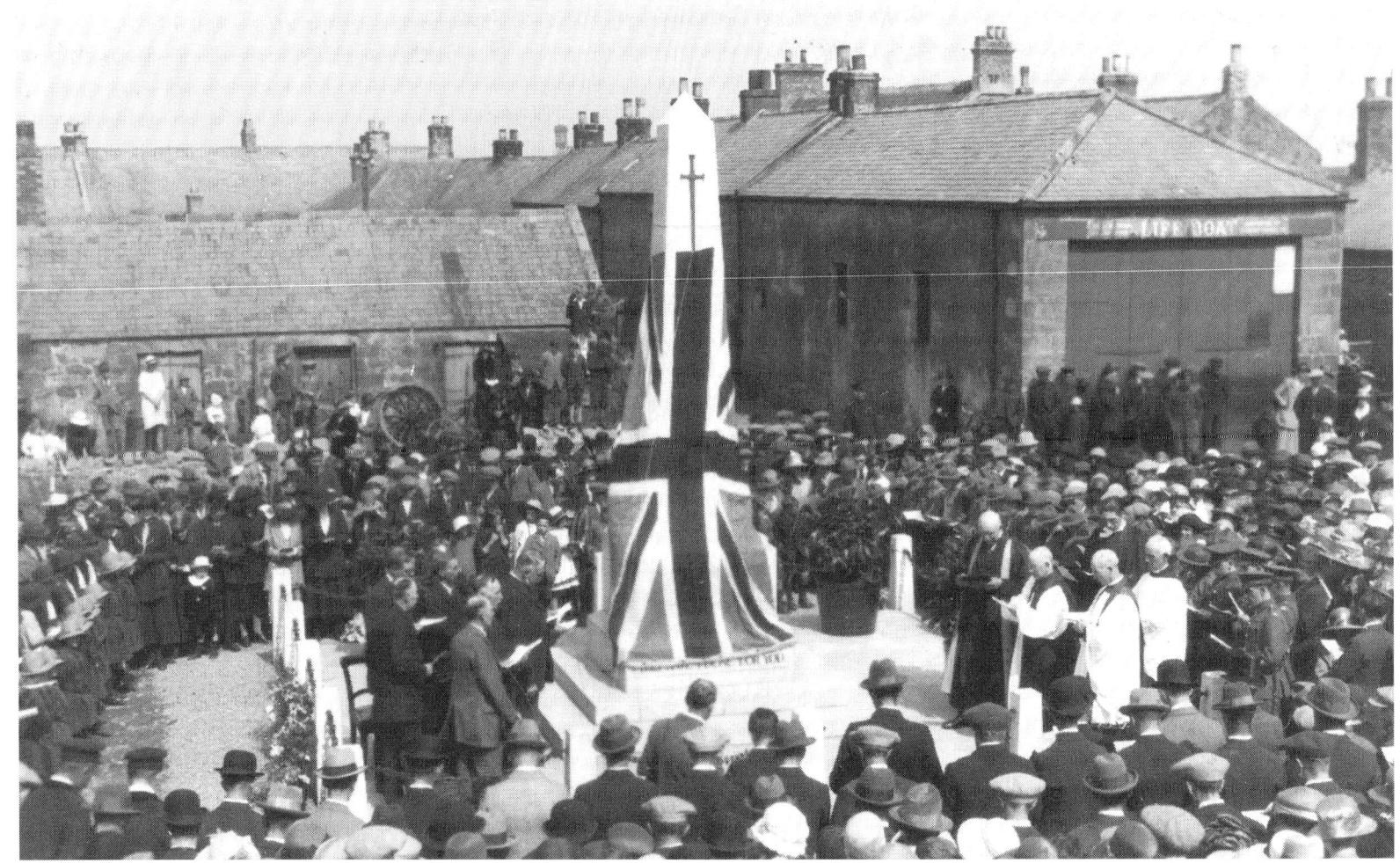

Dedication of the War Memorial, August 5th 1923, presided over by Lord Armstrong, who owned Bamburgh Castle, and Bishop Ormsby, Archdeacon of Lindisfarne. The clergy include Rev. T.H. Berryman (Methodist), Rev. Fred Stone (St. Paul's) and Rev. George Walker (Presbyterian). Additions were made to the memorial after the Second World War. The present roundabout was built around it in 1995, and railings were added to prevent people sitting on it to eat fish and chips. Behind it to the left is Davey Cormack's blacksmith's shop, a hub for both the farming and the fishing industries, demolished in the 1930s as an 'eyesore'. To the right is the old lifeboat house.

649 SHIP HOTEL, SEAHOUSES.

A view from just beyond the old lifeboat house to the harbour, c.1935. On the left is the Reading Room and billiard hall, now part of the Bamburgh Castle Hotel, and the end of 'Lifeboat Raa', cottages which at one time housed workers for Seafield Farm. On the right is the Ship Hotel, one of Seahouses' oldest surviving buildings. It was originally a farmhouse; a lintel of a doorway at the rear carries the date 1745. The Ship has been a public house since 1812, when it was owned by the Hogg family. In 1910 Andrew and Eleanor Lawson, formerly publicans of St. Cuthbert's Inn at Monks' House, became its licensees, and in 1926 they bought the property. The business passed to the Lawsons' descendants, the Glen family, who still run the Olde Ship Hotel as a family business today. Its bars and lounges house an extensive collection of nautical artefacts and memorabilia, and most of the pictures in this book come from the present owner's collection. The original farm stables and coach house remain, although the old farm cottages on the lawn behind the hotel were demolished between the wars. Beneath the hotel sign (right), another sign points to the cinema in the old Methodist chapel.

Main Street, looking west from the War Memorial, *c.*1924. Mayfield Farm is on the left of the picture, with the opening for the old rope railway to the far left, and R. Coxon and Sons Drapers' shop on the right. The development of the north side of Main Street was recent: the 1897 Ordnance Survey plan shows no buildings on that side of the road. Coxons' shop, built in 1900, was the first. Coxons were country tailors who had come to Seahouses from Eglingham in 1896. Their business soon expanded to include small-scale catering for tourists, and that eventually developed into their main business. 'Coxons' Corner', as it is still known locally, now houses the National Trust shop, as well as Coxons' ice cream and coffee bar.

The lane at the back of Mayfield Row cottages, behind Main Street, looking east, *c*.1955, with Nelson Douglas (centre). Mayfield Row (also known as 'Sandy Raa') ran almost down to the Ship Hotel, the chimney of which can be seen in the centre of the picture. The easternmost two houses were two storeys high, and the end one housed Willy Graham's grocer's shop, which was also for a time the post office. The others were single storey, with the farmhouse (not shown) at the west end. These cottages, mostly inhabited by fishermen, had lofts which were used to store herring nets. Each had its own garden, and the southern end of the gardens was separated from farmer Walter Anderson's field by a stone wall, which also included ash 'netties' (privvies) and open middens.

A view from what is now Crumstone estate, looking north over the back of Mayfield Row, c.1921. William and his son Walter Andersons' farm house is among the buildings in the foreground at the far left, and the roof of what is now Barclay's Bank, at that time the Bank of Liverpool and Martin's, can be seen in the background (left). Nellie Fawcus milks a cow (centre) with her brother Harry (left) and their nephew Billy (right). The village farms supplied all the milk required, and cows were walked in from the fields twice a day to be milked. On mart days cattle for sale were walked along the road to Belford. The two little boys on the wall grew up to become well-known fishermen 'Pat' Laidler and Andrew Rutter. Andrew, who was also a talented painter, wrote vividly about his childhood in Mayfield Row in his book, *A Seahouses Saga*.

Mayfield farmer William Anderson with his horse and milk wagon, with Jack Scott at the horse's head, c.1910. This view is also taken from the present Crumstone estate (begun in 1965), but from slightly further west. The Main Street roofline behind it includes (far left) the chimney of Mayfield House, which belonged to the King family, and (far right) the present Barclay's Bank. Adjoining the farmhouse are byres, cart sheds and stabling. The gap between the buildings behind the horse's tail marks the route of Robson and Skelly's old rope-worked incline railway from the quarry to the limekilns. The single storey house to its right was an ale-house and was known as 'Wattie's Corner'.

Jack Scott (with clay pipe) and his team on a break from haymaking in the Seafield Farm fields behind St. Aidan's between the wars. The field is full of hay 'pikes'. Jack Scott worked for farmer Jimmy Smith at Seafield. Behind him is Willie Swan. The woman to the left at the front of the picture wears the traditional costume of a 'bondager', or hired female farm labourer. This ancient form of contract, common in Northumberland and the Borders in the 19th century, was declining by the early 1900s, and disappeared with the organisation of the Women's Land Army in the Second World War.

At the corner of the Ship Hotel, Chapel Row led south past a small butcher's shop, to the first Primitive Methodist chapel, built in 1871. Its roof can be seen here on the left, with a little paddock where Alexander Ewing kept his donkey just in front. Services were held in this chapel until 1926, when the present Methodist church was built on Main Street. This building then became a cinema, with T.B. Gregory's builder's yard (formerly Richard Dawson's herring yard) beside it. Chapel Court now stands next to the site. This photo, taken c.1920, looks north towards the Ship Hotel from an area known as 'the Bullring'. These fishermen's cottages, now extensively renovated, back onto 'Spider Alley'. The woman in the doorway of 'Aa'd Shelly's house' (centre right) is scrubbing her step. The gateway through the wall in the foreground of this picture is known as 'the Nick'. The stones are grooved from generations of fisherwomen, who paused here to sharpen their limpet 'pickers' on the way to the rocks to gather bait for the long lines.

Just to the north of the chapel, out of shot in the top picture, stood the non-denominational 'Piege' (shelter). This L-shaped building was important to community life. It had been a Methodist meeting-room before the first chapel was built, and was also used as a non-sectarian Sunday School. This was run by Presbyterian Alexander Ewing's wife Isabella, then by their descendants. The photo shows Alexander's son James Ewing with a Sunday School outing from Seahouses, probably to Preston, c.1905.

North Street from the bottom of Dunstan View, looking towards the end of Chapel Row, early 1900s. This was the northern edge of the most densely-populated living and working area of the village, made up of numerous herring yards, smokehouses, cooperages and rows and squares of fishermen's cottages. The Dawson family owned the cottages to the left. The little girl (left) is probably Nellie Robson and the man on the right is Mick Fordy. Many of the houses in this area, like those in the centre and to the far right of this photograph, were built as single-storey dwellings and later heightened as families grew wealthier. At this time there were more shops in this part of the village than there were on Main Street. On the left side of the street was George Archbold's Cash Grocery Stores (centre). This was the building in which Seahouses Coop first began. In earlier times it had been a granary, and it later became a fish and chip shop. On the right side was George Roper's bakery (now the Bakehouse B&B). Roper also sold coffee, and hemp fishing lines and hooks. On the same side was another general dealer's, Rachel Robson's. Two old inns dating from the 1830s, the Black Swan and the Schooner, still stand on North Street. The Schooner was originally an ale-house, while the Black Swan, whose entrance is on Union Street, was built c.1834 by Richard Hall, a leading grain merchant, shipping agent and official 'Receiver of Wreck'.

James Ewing's herring yard stood opposite what is now Swallow's fish shop on the corner of South Street and Union Street. Upright and plain-speaking like his father Alexander, James Ewing (right) led many movements for the good of the village, especially in the Presbyterian church, where he was an elder. A staunch Liberal, he first proposed Viscount Grey as M.P. for Berwick on Tweed. James' wife Mary taught Sunday School classes, and kept the books, as well as looking after their seven children. Two of their daughters, Mary and Jeannie, became missionaries in China. As well as fish curing, the Ewings operated a manure and potato business, ensuring that even the fish waste was put to good use. This crew of Ewing's yard includes, *back row, left to right*: Bella Fawcus, Ned Gallagher, Billy McCarthy (with pipe), Jack Swan and John Ewing; *middle row*: Bessie Mitchell, Lizzie Wilson, Nell Dawson, Mary Ann Dawson and in front of her, her daughter, Kate Dawson; Annie Drummond, Isabella Catherine White (Fordy), Mary Swan, Ellen Swan (Patrick). In front are Jim Dawson and (kneeling) John Roper and Bella Graham.

The aftermath of the fire at James Ewing's smokehouse on the corner of South Street and Union Street, 1908. The men include, *left to right*: one of the Braidford family, Ned Allen, Wattie Dunn and John Willie Gregory. A report of this fire from the *Berwick Advertiser* 7th August 1908, perhaps forgetting the events at Seafield in 1844, describes the incident as 'the most serious fire that has probably ever occurred in Seahouses'. The paper goes on to say that other yards, James Boston and Charles Dawson, were also in danger. Mr. Mackenzie of the King Street Inn hurried to Alnwick on a motorcycle to call the fire brigade as there was no telephone in the village. They arrived at 6.30, and the paper reports that the loss was covered by insurance. James Ewing died two years later, in November 1910. The family business ended with him.

Herring lasses in C.W. Dawson's yard, c.1920. R. and C.W. Dawson owned two herring yards in the village. R. Dawson took over one of Alexander Ewing's old yards opposite the Black Swan on Union Street, while this one, C.W. Dawson's, occupied the site that had been Walker's yard and which is now Swallow's smokehouse on South Street. Like much of this area of Seahouses, the buildings originate from the 1830s. In 1877 a writer commented: 'The fishing and fish preserving business together give a rather strong tone to the air at North Sunderland Seahouses.' The women in the picture are packing salt herring; other methods of preserving herring included, traditionally, smoking them for days and even weeks at a time, to produce 'red herrings'. In about 1860, John Woodger, one of a family of Newcastle fish curers, bought property between Union and Taylor Streets, and introduced a new smoking method, called 'kippering'. The herring were split, placed in a bath of brine, then hung in rows on tenterhooks, over oak sawdust fires, and smoked for just 12 hours. Woodger's buildings were demolished in the 1990s, and Swallow's is now the last surviving smokehouse from that proud Seahouses tradition. Kippers may be purchased from the shop which was the kitchen for the herring lasses, who slept in the dormitory above.

W.S. Norris' herring yard stood on the southwest side of Taylor Street, in what had been Woodger's yard. The herring lasses here include (*left to right*): Georgie Ann and Susie Currie, Mary Allen and her mother, Bella Day, Sally Mackenzie, Annie Allen (seated), Mary Jane Norris between Matt Norris and Scottie Richardson, Lily Swan and Bessie Mitchell. The warren of herring yards and warehouses in Taylor Street, Union Street and South Street are now mostly converted into houses, but often retain original features such as arched courtyard entrances, stone setts, and the blocked-up outline of 'bowly holes' in the walls, where cartloads of herring were deposited into sorting troughs called 'farlins'. Farm and fishing cottages were traditionally arranged in 'squares' with open central courtyards. Craster Square in South Street, for example, was an 18th century farm which belonged to the Craster family. The Taylors, after whom Taylor Street is named, were farming landowners who sold land to the Ewings. Sunnieside Square on George Street was converted from herring yards into housing in 1932. It was known as 'Chinatoon' after a popular musical of that name.

Seahouses carter, Jim 'Barber' Douglas (left) with Bill Robson (right), c.1920. Before motor vehicles came into common use between the wars, all transportation in the village, even for the short distance between the harbour and the railway station, was by horse and cart. Thousands of tons of fish were carried this way every year. 'Barber' kept his stables and offices at 'the Flag Yard' on the west side of Union Street, opposite Ewing's old cooperage. The Flag Yard was used to dry the Coastguard flags, which some maintain accounts for its name. Others suggest that this was derived from flagstones brought from Scotland as ballast and stored there, or from its flagstone floor. When Barber's horses were replaced by motor wagons, he parked his vehicles at 'the Cement' at the top of Union Street, where he also ran the local scrapyard – a favourite adventure playground for the village children.

Lance Turnbull (left) outside his general dealer's, grocer's and ironmonger's shop on the north side of Main Street, c.1930. Many of the houses and shops on the street were built in the first decade of the 20th century in the distinctive local red and yellow sandstone, which has blackened over the years. Turnbull's business had begun in North Sunderland and moved to Seahouses as the village prospered. Ethel Craig stands in the doorway (centre), with Mary (Allen) Kilbourne who did the office-work (right). Mary and her husband later took over the shop, which became D. and M.E. Kilbourne's grocers'. The village continued to evolve and expand, undergoing further alterations to Main Street in the early 1970s, when the old Mayfield Farm buildings on the south side were demolished and replaced with amusement arcades, of which Johnny's was the first. The character of the village changed considerably at that time, as the caravan sites expanded, nightclubs opened in the Dolphin and Viking restaurants above the harbour, and fish and chip shops and the new gambling and gaming machines proliferated. Traditionally Methodist and Presbyterian, much of the older generation in Seahouses was uncomfortable with these changes, and the letters pages of local newspapers expressed concerns that the village, no longer 'the Yarmouth of the North', would become instead 'the Las Vegas of the North'.

Main Street looking east towards the lifeboat house in the mid 1920s. At the far left is Jarrett's baker's shop, later Hall's. Next to it stands Lily Gladstone House, for a time Miss Orde's post office, and now the chemist, and Helena House, which was at this time a smallholding. These date from 1903. At the far right is Young's Tea Room and Guesthouse, with its bakery round the back. The painted outline of the name 'Young's' is still faintly legible today. The next building visible to its left is the Manse. This was built before the new Primitive Methodist Chapel, which opened for worship in 1926. St. Aidan's House, now an hotel, served as an earlier manse. It is not possible to see from this angle whether the Chapel has been built, because it is set back from the road. The new Chapel was funded by the local community, including a generous gift of £4,500 from Sir Walter and Lady Runciman of Shoreston Hall. Christianity of many denominations was, and remains, a central part of village life, with the Chapel a hub of community activity to this day.

Seahouses Fishermen's Choir began in the Methodist Chapel in 1950. Inspired by a Scottish fishermen's choir he heard at Yarmouth, Richard Dawson helped found it, together with its first member Jack 'Dobbin' Robson. It quickly caught on as a community group, raising money to support the Chapel and the RNLI, and was popular for its renditions of favourite maritime hymns, especially those from the Sankey and Moody hymn book. Seen here in 1951, the choir includes, *left to right*: Andrew Rutter, Tom Dawson, George Nelson, Tom Gregory, Charlie 'Carl' Dawson, George 'Ginger' Dawson, Bob Borthwick, George Shorthouse, Billy Shiel, Andrew Liddell, Richard Nelson, Herbert Gallagher, Charlie Dawson, Mick Robson, Rev. Staton (minister), Norman Archbold, Pat Laidler, George Dawson, Jack Shiel, Tom Baxter Douglas, ? Ronnie Rawlings (obscured), Tom Robinson, Bobby Douglas, Gordon Archbold, Tom Hall (obscured), George Dawson Jr, Tony Hall, Jim Trotter, Richard Dawson, Jack 'Dobbin' Robson, Douggie Hall, John Thorburn, John Archbold. With the decline of fishing in Seahouses, the Fishermen's Choir was disbanded in 2004, and superseded by Village Voices, a mixed community choir.

Front Street, Sea Houses.

Main Street looking east from what is now the top roundabout, c.1919, with Jeffray's stationery and newsagent's shop on the left. Out of sight, further to the left was Fender's garage. In the centre, from *left to right*, are Mayfield House, the Manse and Young's Tea Room and Longstone guesthouse, with a wall in front of Young's. The bakery was at the back. Centre right is the brick building which housed North Sunderland and Seahouses Cooperative Society and still serves as the Coop today. This was originally built as two semi-detached houses. It is said that the bricks were brought from the colliery at Amble by fishing boat. Annie Dawson's shop occupied one of the houses before it became the Cooperative. To the far right, on the corner, is Jubilee House, named for Queen Victoria's Jubilee in 1897. This is now also part of the Coop supermarket, but was at that time a shoemaker's and cobbler's house and shop, belonging to Jacob Matthews and his son Charlie Wully. Their shop front was around the corner. Matthews made leather sea-boots for the local fishermen.

Another view from a little further up the street, taken a few years earlier. The occasion is not known. The photograph shows few buildings on the north side of the road. Mayfield House, enlarged from a single-storey cottage by the King family, stands alone (centre left). Hay's herring yard is out of shot to the rear. The Kings, Hays and Ewings were all related by marriage. At the centre of the picture are Young's and the semi-detached houses which became the Coop and, on the right, the King Street Inn, which occupied the site which later became the Farne Hotel. West of King Street, on the south side of the road, next to what is now Scott's butcher's shop, there was another large herring yard, Browns', with houses above part of it fronting the street, approached by outside stone stairs and a landing. There was an ale-house called The Badger Inn in what is now 75 Main Street, next to the footpath to Kippy Law – one of the few houses in the village with a cellar.

Another view of the King Street Inn, taken from across the road, where C.W. Matthews had his boot and shoe shop. The King Street Inn had outbuildings attached to it, and the publican R.W. Mackenzie kept a paint shop there. The three children at the centre of the picture are, *left to right*: Annie, Roderick and Edward Mackenzie. R.W. Mackenzie owned shares in Newcastle United Football Club from when it was founded in 1892, and began the club's long association with Seahouses, which continues to this day. It is said that the first turf for the club's St. James' Park ground was cut from Annstead Burn. Opposite the King Street Inn, on Main Street, were three houses and a garden. These were demolished together with the Inn when the corner and King Street (known locally as the Beadnell Road) were altered c.1930. The Farne Hotel, the distinctive building on the corner which today houses a beautician's and coffee shop, was built in place of the King Street Inn and was intended to resemble the bridge of a ship. King Street is named after Thomas King, who was harbour master in the mid 19th century, and whose son William owned a herring yard. The Kings were related to the Ewings and, like them, built a lot of property in Seahouses. There were no further houses on King Street between the King Street Inn and Kippy Law Farm until the 1930s.

Main Street, Seahouses.   M. 504.

Main Street, looking west towards North Sunderland, between the wars. There are no houses on the left (south) side of the street running up to the cemetery. The fields to the south were named Kippy Law and Stone Close, and those names were retained by the housing estates built on them after the war. Seahouses County Secondary School, now the Middle School, was also built on land south of Main Street, and opened in 1961. The pair of gates on the right led to the Drill Hall, which was built for the 2nd Northumberland Volunteer Artillery, part of the volunteer force established in 1859 following the Crimean War. It was also used for social events. On the 1897 Ordnance Survey map the Drill Hall was the only building on the north side of the road until the police station in North Sunderland (centre). Beside the police station stood one of the early village wells. Clean drinking water was scarce: cholera broke out in the village in the early 1800s. In 1832 residents petitioned the Lord Crewe Trustees for a water pump. The pump and water-tower at Seafield were installed soon afterwards (p.13).

Looking east down Main Street, with what is now Seahouses First School on the left. The sign on the road to the right points to it. North Sunderland Council School opened on 25th September 1906 on land given by the Lord Crewe Trust. It cost £2,690 to build, was maintained by the local education authority and accommodated 250 children aged five to 14. The Council School replaced the Lord Crewe Trust's Boys' and Girls' schools in North Sunderland and the Infants' in the Bamburgh Castle Inn. James Ewing was Chairman of the School Managers. It became a primary school in 1961 when the secondary school opened. In its grounds stands a whalebone arch, acquired from a local farmer in 1938, which is thought to be one of the best-preserved in the region. Behind the school stood the Comrades' Institute (now the Working Men's Club), erected by subscription in memory of men who fought in the First World War. The gate between the school and the Comrades' Institute was known as the 'Fishers' Gate' from the time when most fishermen lived away from the shore, some say to escape excise men and press gangs.

Opposite: The headmaster of North Sunderland Council School from 1906 to 1929 was Fordyce Welch (right, with a class *c.*1920). Welch, a strict disciplinarian, lived to be 101. At the time of this picture, children from the outlying farms such as Pasture Hill, Elford and Springhill, walked several miles to school every day carrying their 'bait tin' and tea in a bottle. One teacher, Miss Milliken, cycled from Chathill. Although by 1906 school attendance had been compulsory for a generation, the log book from the new school records that many children were still kept away by their parents to help with the herring catch, in the fields or with boarders. In 2006-7 Seahouses First School celebrated its centenary with a number of projects marking the changes in the settlement over that 100 years, from a fishing and farming community to a much larger village focused on the tourist and holiday industries. While many older residents felt that the village was no longer as closely-knit as it once was, all agreed that the school plays a vital role in uniting it and retaining its distinctive character and identity.

North Sunderland, looking east down Main Street from Hastings' Farm (right, now demolished), c.1910. North Sunderland predates Seahouses by many centuries. It consists of Main Street, with North and South Lane running on either side of it. Hastings' farmhouse stood next to the church. The Dairy Farm and slate-roofed 'Blue Row' farm cottages stand in the centre of the picture. East of these was the Masonic Hall. Opposite the farm on the north side was Davey Brown's grocer's shop, and the Jolly Tar ale-house. Further along was the boys' school with its distinctive sundial; it later became the Ex-Servicemen's club, then the Lodge Inn and is now holiday accommodation. At the far right of the picture is a shop and post office, and near the centre, Railston's Granaries, which were used for dances and as a drill hall. Railston House (out of sight) was home to the wealthiest man in 19th century Seahouses, land-owner, grain merchant and money-lender, John Railston. His daughter, disappointed in love, ended her days alone, and after her death, it is said, her house was found stuffed full of money. On South Lane, at the back of Hastings' Farm, was an old school. North Sunderland had four farms, Hastings', Dairy Farm, Village or Home Farm (Smiths') and Slate Hall (Murdues'). Tracks led across the fields from South Lane to what is now the golf course and the Burn Sands. These were known as 'Crewie Lonnen', which became 'Cowie Lonnen'; and 'the Ware Road', once used by kelp-gatherers collecting seaweed ('ware'), which was spread on the fields as fertiliser.

St. Paul's Anglican Church c.1914, with the old Parsonage (since demolished) to the left. St. Paul's Church was built by the Lord Crewe Trustees in 1833-4, after North Sunderland separated from Bamburgh Parish. It occupies the site of an earlier pele tower, which was two storeys high, with walls five feet thick. The tower served a defensive purpose during raids by the Scots, and in the Civil War it was attacked by cannon fire. When it was demolished, cannon balls were found and a hoard of 17th century coins was discovered hidden inside it. The church was built by Anthony Salvin, the renowned architect who worked on the restoration of Bamburgh and Alnwick Castles, and who built the Grace Darling Memorial in Bamburgh and St. Paul's Church in Alnwick. Members of Grace Darling's family are buried in St. Paul's Churchyard. There is also a memorial to seven men and boys who lost their lives in the coal mine at Pasture Hill 'by a sudden influx of water' on 7th October 1843. A few years before the church was built, the Lord Crewe Trust opened a new Church of England school in the building opposite. To begin with, this was a mixed school with 34 pupils, of whom seven were free. It soon became the girls' school, while the boys were educated down the road in The Lodge. The building now serves as St. Paul's Hostel, catering to groups of visitors.

Main Street, North Sunderland, looking west, c.1920. The shop on the right was at that time the post office (now a curio shop). Next to it, set back from the road, were tennis courts, a garden and the Village ('Home') Farm. Prior to mechanisation, farms employed a large number of male and female labourers. At Alnwick hirings in March 1907, a 'hind' who brought with him a woman worker and a young lad, could command 18s or 19s per week. Women were paid 1s 6d per day, with 3s per day for 20 days in harvest. To the left of this picture is Milestone House, the former Manor House Granary, standing one mile from Seahouses Harbour. The milestone, which marks one mile from the end of the pier, is now incorporated into the wall. Behind it, set back from the road, is the oldest building in the village, Croft House, formerly the Manor House, part of which dates from c.1650. It became the Blue Bell Inn in the early 1800s. A Bronze Age burial cist (c.1,500-500 BC) containing the body of a young girl was found while digging a drain here in 1862. Three pottery vessels were discovered at the same time. One was broken; the other two are now in the British Museum.

North Sunderland looking west towards the Manse and the 'High' Presbyterian Chapel, built 1810 (centre). This was one of two Presbyterian chapels in North Sunderland, the other being on North Lane. The 'High' Chapel is now St. Cuthbert's House B&B. Today the Presbyterian congregation shares St. Paul's Anglican Church. The pan-tiled, or possibly thatched, cottage to the right of the chapel was Fender's Smithy. Fender later had a garage on the west end of Main Street in Seahouses. One of the other cottages was a dairy. The telegraph post marks the Broad Road end, with the wall of the White Swan in the foreground (right). The buildings to the left were, *left to right*: Tom Tait's boot and shoe maker (later a post office), R. Scott the butcher (whose killing shop was at the end of the garden onto South Lane), and Lance Turnbull's grocer's shop. Turnbull later moved his business to Seahouses (p.35).

"WHITE SWAN" AND "WARWICK HOUSE." NORTH SUNDERLAND.

The White Swan (proprietor J. Anderson) and Warwick House, which was occupied in the mid 20th century by the Hughes family, c.1920. The White Swan was originally a thatched building. Like many in the village, it was heightened. It became Longstone House Hotel and is now in private hands. At the north end of Warwick House was Cathcart's saddler's shop, which later moved into the shop facing the King Street corner of Main Street in Seahouses, and a cottage occupied by an old lady, Lizzie Arnott. To the east of these buildings along the road was J. Walton's general dealers. Also in this area was stabling for Davey Brown's horse. Behind this side of Main Street, on North Lane, stood the old Presbyterian Manse, dating from 1810, together with the 'Low' Presbyterian Church and a farm steading. At the other end of North Lane, on Barclay's Corner, was another saddler's shop and a scrap iron business.

North Sunderland Station and railway crossing, on the Broad Road near the road to Springhill Farm. The Broad Road runs across the picture. Part of the station platform can still be seen in the grounds of the household waste recovery centre. The Swanson family lived in the house next to the platform (right). Maggie Swanson was the crossing keeper. The train blew its whistle for the crossing gates to be opened, three times in the morning and three in the afternoon. Before the First World War many people did not own a watch, so they told the time by it, even when at sea. Today a little plantation marks the beginning of the cycleway to Seahouses, which runs along the old railway line. A small industrial estate lies just beyond it.

462. THE HUTS AND SANDS, SEAHOUSES.

Throughout the 19th century Seahouses attracted wealthy visitors – often naturalists and artists – taking boat trips to the Farne Islands. The holiday industry began to develop in the 1920s, with greater mobility brought about by railway travel. At that time there were few local hotels, and they catered for affluent visitors. Most holidaymakers stayed at local inns or took 'lodgings' with fishing families. After the Second World War, the motor car became the main means of transport. To cater for more mobile holidaymakers, caravan sites were opened, first to the south and later to the north of the village, and local families offered guesthouse and bed and breakfast accommodation. Today, Seahouses' population rises from approximately 1,800 to around three times that number during the high season. This picture, c.1930, shows beach huts, which remained until after the Second World War, and a sand dune, known locally as 'Fat-Belly Hill', which is part of St. Aidan's Dunes, stretching to Greenhill and including Monks' House, ¾ of a mile to the north. This land was conveyed to the National Trust by the Lord Crewe Trustees in 1936 as a result of the generosity of Sir Walter Runciman of Shoreston Hall and others.

The Dunes Hotel c.1936. The original central part of The Dunes was built in 1914 by Captain and Mrs. Buddle-Atkinson of the Bolam Estate outside Newcastle. At that time it stood alone on St. Aidan's, opposite an early lime-burning site known as 'the Far Kilns'. The other houses north of Seafield Farm were built between the wars, as the rather exclusive 'St. Aidan's by the Sea'. The West Wing of The Dunes was added as servants' quarters when the house became a permanent residence, and a glass-house was built on the northeast corner to accommodate pet monkeys. One night one of the monkeys escaped from The Dunes, and climbed a telegraph pole outside. Shortly afterwards they were given to Edinburgh Zoo. The Dunes opened as a Private Hotel in 1933. The East Wing extension (Farne Court) was added in 1939. About the time of this picture, Mary, Duchess of Bedford, stayed at the hotel to study birds on the Farne Islands. She had recently obtained her pilot's licence at the age of 68, and was only prevented by startled livestock from landing her Moth Major in an adjacent field. Less than a year later she was killed in a flying accident over the North Sea. During the war, while other local hotels were requisitioned by the military, the Dunes remained open, and it had many distinguished guests before it closed for business in 1982. The building is now three separate properties, The Dunes, the Dunes West Wing and Farne Court.

Opposite: Monks' House in St. Aidan's Dunes north of Seahouses, *c*.1900. A charter of 1257 gave land at 'Brocksmouth' to the monks of Farne to build a granary. The building was used for stores to supply a small Benedictine cell of one or two monks from Durham Priory who lived on Inner Farne from the mid 13th century until the dissolution of the monasteries *c*.1540. The sandy haven at Monks' House was more suitable for cobles than the rocky Seahouses shore, so it long pre-dated Seahouses as a fishing place. In 1626 'Shoreston and North Sunderland' had seven resident fishermen, who kept their boats here. Monks' House was also reputed to be a refuge for smugglers. The current buildings are mostly early 19th century, and the house served as St. Cuthbert's Inn. This picture shows Andrew Lawson and his family, licensees, *c*.1900. After the restoration of Bamburgh Castle, when the Irish itinerant labouring trade moved away, business declined, and the Lawsons moved to the Ship Hotel in Seahouses. Monks' House was later used as a bird observatory and field centre by the writer and artist Eric Ennion.

A genteel lady from Sir John Craster's family visits Inner Farne, *c*.1900. The 'cuddy' (donkey), which belonged to Trinity House and lived on the island, was used for carrying heavy loads. Although now uninhabited except for seasonal wardens, the island was at the time home to three lighthouse keepers and their families. Inner Farne has a long tradition of habitation. St. Cuthbert lived there as a hermit, and died there in 687AD. He was succeeded by other hermits, and from 1250 until *c*.1540, by the formal cell mentioned above. Among their written records are accounts of fishing gear, including cobles, long lines and herring nets. St. Cuthbert's Chapel (centre) was built in the 14th century. Behind it are the ruins of a pele tower, built *c*.1500 for Thomas Castell, Prior of Durham. The first wardens were installed on the Farne Islands in the late 19th century by ornithologists who, anxious to deter egg collectors, leased the islands from the estate of Archdeacon Thorp. The islands were subsequently bought by subscription and vested in the National Trust in 1925. They remain an important wildlife sanctuary for puffins, Arctic terns and grey seals, and attract thousands of visitors from Seahouses every year.

A sailing coble, Inner Farne, *c*.1900. There are between 15 and 20 Farne Islands, depending on the tide. Scattered 1½–4¾ miles from the mainland, they are divided into the Inner and Outer islands. The site of countless wrecks, especially in the days of sail, the islands have two working lighthouses, now automatic: Inner Farne (1811), and Longstone Lighthouse (1826). Longstone is famous for the story of Grace Darling, who on 7th September 1838, at the age of 22, assisted her father, William, the lighthouse keeper, in the rescue of nine people from the wreck of the *Forfarshire* which had run aground on Harcar Rock. The coble in which Grace and her father effected the rescue was not unlike the one in this picture. A few years earlier, on 2nd February 1823, William Darling's journal records the loss of three vessels with all hands on the rocks in an easterly gale and snowstorm. Although a grave danger to shipping, the islands have also served as a place of sanctuary. In a sudden blizzard on February 6th 1895, many local cobles sought safety there; and on November 17th 1962, the crew of Seahouses fishing boat *Faithful II*, together with those of the Seahouses and Holy Island lifeboats, were lifted by RAF helicopter onto Inner Farne, where they spent two nights.

The Beadnell Road from the end of King Street, looking north from the golf course, c.1938. The 1925 Ordnance Survey map shows few houses on King Street, with only the Kippy Law farm buildings between the King Street Inn and the row of rendered limestone houses (far left). These houses, originally single storey, were built as granaries for John Railston in the early 19th century. They were known as 'Muslin Raa', after a shipload of muslin came ashore at the Burn Sands and was dried and stored there. The houses in the centre of the picture were also originally single-storey granaries. Dunstan View is just visible centre right. In the 18th and 19th centuries Snook Point, to the east, owned by the Lord Crewe Estates, was an industrial area, with coal shafts and windmill pump-engines, clay pits, Robson and Skelly's limestone quarries, and Ewing's herring refuse processing plant, which was situated on the north edge of the quarry. A horse-drawn wagonway ran along the west side of the granaries, carrying limestone to the harbour kilns, and the rope-operated railway ran across what is now the golf course to the east. Trains were hauled up tramways by a rope from the engine house above, then sent by gravity down a long incline to the kilns at the harbour. The 'gut' at the end of the golf course was used as a haven for sloops exporting the local red sandstone quarried from the shore. In August 1844 workers at the quarry discovered an underground chamber: a cave with a flagstone floor, and a ventilation shaft connected to a cottage built above it. The cave was probably a hiding place for smuggled goods landed at the Burn Sands on the south beach. The present 18-hole golf course was originally a nine-hole course founded in 1913.

North Sunderland Football Club *c*.1932. This very old established club was a member of the North Northumberland League, and won the Mackenzie Cup three years in succession before 1914, then again in 1923-4. It also won the Alnwick Infirmary Sanderson Cup in 1926-7 and 1935-6. *Back row, left to right*: John W. Gregory, John Gregory, Jimmy Douglas, George Bertram, Willie Swan, Ralphie Dawson, Danny Cormack. *Front row*: Jack Shiel, 'Kelpie' Bill Robson, Tommy Gregory, Bobby Douglas, Bill Robson, Robert 'Barty' Bertram. Jack Shiel (bottom left) went on to be a professional footballer. When he died in 2013 at the age of 96, he was the last surviving pre-war Newcastle United and Huddersfield Town player. His footballing career was cut short by the Second World War, and he returned to fishing after serving aboard minesweepers. What is now Mitchell Avenue was a cart track to 'the Acres', seven fields of differing sizes. The field now occupied by Megstone Close served for a time as the village football field.